TULLY AND THE MAKEOVER

Available in the Tales of Tully series

Tully's Life
This heart-warming story follows the journey of Tully from street dog to much-loved family pet, teaching young readers about the importance of kindness, understanding and hope.

Tully Takes Off!
Tully has arrived in her new home with her new grown-up, but she does not like it one bit! When Tully sees an opportunity to go back to her old life on the streets - the only life she has known up to now - she takes it with both paws. With a search underway, it is up to her new grown-up to work out what Tully needs and help get her safely home.

Tully and the Sad Day
Tully has woken up feeling grey and cloudy inside and she does not know what to do. She cannot help her big feeling because she does not know what it is. As her different feelings begin to work together in the wrong way, it is up to Tully's grown-up to help her to understand what she needs.

Go To Sleep Tully!
It is night time and Tully is tired, but she does not want to go to sleep. Her new grown-up knows that Tully is trying every trick she can to avoid going go to bed! With lots of adventures planned and Tully needing her rest, Tully's grown-up needs to find a way to help Tully learn to not be so worried about bedtime.

Tully and the Midnight Feast
Tully is a newly-adopted dog settling in with her new grown-up. Since her arrival, her snacks have started mysteriously disappearing from the cupboard and appearing under her bed, she seems to have forgotten her manners, and there are days when she just cannot stop eating! Tully and her grown-up need to work together to help Tully with her worries about food.

Tully and the Scary Day
Tully has woken up feeling scared. She isn't really sure why, but today feels like a very scary day, and she just wants to hide. Tully's grown-up is thankfully there to help Tully manage her big feelings and see that the day is not so scary after all.

Don't Touch Tully!
Tully is settling in with her new grown-up. She has learned that the new grown-up is a safe person and she enjoys strokes and cuddles with them. Then Tully starts to meet new people, who want to show her how loved she is. Unfortunately, Tully doesn't feel the same about people she does not know and trust. It is up to Tully's grown-up to find a way to help Tully with her big feelings and to be Tully's voice, when she can't use hers.

Tully and the Tummy Ache
Tully has a tummy ache and it's making her feel quite grumpy. She doesn't want to eat or drink, and she can't get comfortable. Her tummy is sore and it's getting worse! Tully is in a toilet muddle. So, Tully and her grown-up work together to sort the muddle out and help Tully to cure her tummy ache.

Tully's Birthday
It's Tully's birthday, and her grown-up has planned a special day for her, but Tully doesn't feel like celebrating. As the day begins to unfold, so do Tully's big feelings. Tully doesn't know what to do about the big feelings, so she does a bad thing. Luckily, Tully's grown-up is there to help her feel better about herself, and enjoy the rest of her birthday.

Listen, Tully!
Tully does not always like to listen, especially when her grown-up is trying to stop her having fun. Tully decides that instead of listening, she can be in charge. But when things start to go wrong, Tully and her grown-up need to work out how Tully can begin to find listening a little bit easier.

Tully and the Makeover
Tully has been having lots of fun playing in the mud, but now her grown-up says she has to have a bath. Oh dear! Tully is not sure she wants one of those. She is feeling a bit nervous about what is going to happen to her, but Tully's grown-up shows her that there is nothing to worry about. Having a bath is a good thing after all.

Tully and Vera
Tully has moved in with her new grown-up but she is missing her foster carer, Vera. Tully is struggling to understand why she had to leave, and whether it is okay to have big feelings about Vera. It is up to Tully's grown-up to try and help her to understand loss and endings and why, sometimes, they have to happen to make space for new beginnings.

Tully and the Chase
Tully loves to be chased. It gives her a feeling of excitement which starts off as being fun, but one day the excited feeling suddenly and very quickly becomes a feeling which is too big. Instead of feeling excited, Tully starts to feel scared. Tully and her grown-up need to work out how they can play Tully's exciting game without it becoming a bit too much for her, and causing a muddle.

Tully at Christmas
Things are starting to feel a bit different in Tully's house and all around outside. Tully's grown-up looks different, strange lights are appearing everywhere and people have started putting their gardens indoors! Tully is not sure what to make of this thing called Christmas - she just wants everything to stay the same. What can Tully's grown-up do to make Christmas-time a nicer time for both of them?

Tully Goes on Holiday
Tully has gone on a holiday with her grown-up. After a difficult start, things seem to be going well. But when the fairground opens up, with all its flashing lights, loud music and food smells, Tully's big feelings get the better of her, making her want to run. And she does! Tully's grown-up needs to find her in time to show her that holidays can be fun after all.

Tully and the New Rules
Tully likes lots of things about living in a house with her grown-up, but one thing she really doesn't like is all the rules! Tully thinks the rules are all very boring and her grown-up must want to stop her from having fun. One day Tully breaks her least favourite rule, and something bad happens. Tully doesn't know what to do! Can Tully's grown-up get to the bottom of this muddle so it doesn't happen again?

Tully and the Makeover

TALES OF TULLY

Jess van der Hoech

Trauma Tools
& Training

ISBN-13 978-1-06-86917-5-1
Editing by Sarah Ogden
www.jvtraumatools.co.uk

Acknowledgements

As always, to my trusted editor Sarah Ogden for all that you do to make these books come to life. I will never fully know what goes on behind the scenes, but it is a joy to work alongside you on these projects. Thank you.

Thank you to my supervisor Linda Hoggan for your continued support, encouragement, discussion and much-welcomed feedback on this series. I learn so much from you and the knowledge I have gained form our conversations has been invaluable across my practice, the books and now this series. Thank you.

Thank you to Laura Benham, for your support in giving me feedback, the searching questions, your friendship and of course, the countless conversations about dogs, the content of which has become quite useful! Thank you.

To the children and families who I meet in my therapy room, from whom I have learned more about hope and healing than any course could ever teach me. Your input, ideas, questions and answers are so valuable to me and I will be forever grateful. Thank you.

Preface

The *Tales of Tully* series is based on the adoption of an ex street dog from Bosnia who came to live with me in September 2023. Watching her try to settle and adapt from everything she had previously known to fit in with a new way of life began to present a number of ideas as to how to communicate such difficulties that can be experienced, to others who are in the process of adopting or who have adopted children. The aim of the series is to provide an opportunity to explore different situations, circumstances, feelings and experiences, finding new ways of communicating and understanding each other, through the voice of Tully.

The first time I put Tully in the bath to shower her, after toileting through fear, she physically shut down and collapsed in the bath. She had to have a wash as she had wet her bed and been laying in it and so the shower was a necessity. She simply did not know what it was and it sent her fear levels rocketing. After she was washed and came out of the bath in a towel, she began to settle, back in her bed which was her safe place then, knowing that she was safe again.

She enjoyed being brushed afterwards, her claws being clipped, not so much! So, as it was not a matter of urgency, I left claw clipping for a while.

A few weeks after this, Tully developed a skin condition; she was patchy and losing hair and seemed to constantly be scratching. I took her to the vets who knew that this was a mild complaint and could easily be treated with a special shampoo that needed to be applied six times in total – twice a week, at the minimum.

I was terrified. I knew that Tully had hated the bath and now I had to get her in it twice a week! However, the first treatment was not as bad as the first bath had been, and she accepted what we were doing and with a lovely massage of the shampoo, I would go so far as to say she actually enjoyed it a bit. She must have felt better for it and knew that the baths were helping her, because as the schedule went on, there was less and less resistance. By the time the treatment was complete, the skin condition had gone and I had a much happier and less itchy Tully.

It made me reflect on how many times I see issues around self-care in the therapy room with children; the most common complaint – not brushing their teeth! Bathing and grooming is a very sensory experience, some people love it and some don't. It is important to think about what the resistance to some self-care could be. For example, with teeth cleaning – has the child learned how to clean their teeth properly? Are they using the correct amount of toothpaste? Is the flavour of the toothpaste too strong? Are the bristles of the tooth brush too hard and almost painful? For a child who struggles to brush their teeth, setting the recommended two minute timer is too much! Start with thirty seconds, twenty or even ten and build the time up as they begin to get used to it.

Children who have had early trauma may have had painful experiences with teething if they were never given any pain relief or comfort. Poor hygiene practices may have led to tooth decay, meaning that anything oral is now linked to pain. By considering all of these potential issues with all forms of self-care, plans can be put in place that meet the child's needs. Teeth cleaning, bathing, showering, hair brushing, nails being cut – all of these things have the potential to be triggering experiences for the child.

Through the story of Tully, children may be able to give more information and clues as to why they may find such experiences difficult, meaning that plans can be put in place to help ease this, making self-care more manageable for the grown up and child.

How to use this book

First and foremost, ensure that both you and the child are well-regulated and comfortable when you begin to read Tully's story. Make sure you choose a time when you are unlikely to be interrupted. The child may like a soother, a favourite or fidget toy, a drink or something to suck or chew to help them to stay regulated.

If the child is calm, then begins to try and distract or move away from the reading, make a note of what they have just heard in the text. It is very likely that they will have just provided you with some valuable information about something that they cannot tolerate or want to avoid for now.

The questions have been designed not only to explore the internal world of the child, but to help to develop a common language between the child and adult who are using this book together. The child cannot get the answers to the questions incorrect. Their interpretation of the thoughts and feelings Tully is having may provide some very significant information about the child's own thoughts and feelings. The child may want to expand the answers to talk about themselves and may even be able to make comparisons between Tully's feelings and their own.

Tully and the Makeover

Tully was outside playing in the garden. She loved it in the garden. There were lots of things for her to smell, and Tully loved to sniff.

Tully found a scent in the lawn. She sniffed around the ground. "What's that?" she wondered.

Tully used her paw to scratch away the surface of the grass to really smell the smell. Tully discovered a dog treat she must have left in the garden a while ago that had been covered over by the grass. As Tully scratched at the lawn, she also discovered that she liked the feeling of mud on her paws.

Do you like playing outdoors?

What things do you like the feeling of?

Tully started to dig. She dug, and she dug. The hole got bigger and bigger – big enough for Tully to put her head into. There was a pile of mud next to where Tully had been digging. Tully rolled in it. It felt great! Tully loved mud rolling! She was having a lovely time.

"What are you doing Tully?!" her grown-up said. Tully had been rolling around so much she had not heard her grown-up come outside.

"Look at the state of you! What a mess!" her grown-up said.

How is Tully feeling?

Tully did not know what her grown-up meant. She was only having some fun.

Tully looked down at her paws. They usually had white patches on them. Today, they were brown. In fact her legs were a different colour too.

Tully started to itch. She started scratching all over as hard as she could, where the mud had begun to irritate her skin.

"I think you need a bath," Tully's grown-up said.

Tully was horrified. A bath! She did not want one of those!

How might Tully feel about having a bath?

What are the good things about having a bath?

Are there any things that are not so good about having a bath?

Tully heard her grown-up in the bathroom filling the bath with water. Tully went to look. When she got into the bathroom, a terrible thing happened – her grown-up shut the door! Tully was trapped!

"In you get Tully, let's get the worst of the mud off, then I can shower you." Tully did not know what this meant so she did not get in. She stayed put!

Is it a good idea for Tully to get in the bath?

Why does Tully need to have a wash?

What might her worries be?

Tully's grown-up picked her up and gently put her into the bath. Tully took a minute to notice the feelings of being in the water.

How might the water feel to Tully?

How do you feel when you have a bath or shower?

Tully's grown-up gently poured the water over her and then rubbed some sweet-smelling shampoo into her muddy fur. Tully liked the feeling of the shampoo being rubbed onto her.

Next, Tully's grown-up used the shower to rinse the shampoo off Tully.

The plug on the bath was pulled and the dirty water began to drain away. Tully thought she was going to go down the plughole with the dirty water, but Tully's grown-up reminded her that she was much too big to go down the plughole.

The grown-up continued to rinse Tully until the water ran clear.

How might Tully feel now she is clean?

Tully got out of the bath and her grown-up wrapped her in a soft, warm towel. They went downstairs and sat together on the sofa.

Tullys grown-up took her paw from under the towel and showed Tully something she had not seen before.

"These are called clippers, Tully. They're for your long claws," the grown-up told her.

Tully did not want her claws clipped off!

How might Tully feel about having her claws clipped?

Why is it important that her claws do not get too long?

Tully did not want her claws clipped; it gave her a worried feeling. What if it hurt?

Snip – the first claw was trimmed. "Oh! That was okay," thought Tully and so she stayed still while the rest of her claws were cut.

When Tully put her paws on the floor, they felt much better now her long claws were not in the way. When Tully scratched behind her ear, it felt much better and did not hurt like it sometimes did when she scratched herself with her long claws.

Tully's grown-up then started to brush her fur.

How does Tully feel about having her fur brushed?

Why is it important for Tully to have her fur brushed?

Finally, Tully's grown-up gave her a special stick to chew on that would clean Tully's teeth.

Why is it important for Tully to have healthy teeth?

"There! Look at you!" the grown-up said, looking proudly at Tully. Lovely clean skin and fur, brushed and shiny, claws clipped and teeth cleaned. Tully felt amazing!

Her makeover had not been so bad after all. Tully was not scared of the bath anymore.

So she went outside and dug another hole.

About the author

Jess van der Hoech is a qualified therapist who has spent the last ten years studying and working with the impact of developmental trauma and, in particular, the assessment and treatment of children and adolescents with complex trauma and dissociation.

As well as supporting birth families, Jess works with looked-after and adopted children and families, using skills in attachment-focused therapy and therapeutic parenting techniques.

Jess is a supervisor, trainer and motivational speaker with a passion for writing therapeutic books that are accessible to children and families to help with the healing process and to increase awareness in the impact of trauma.

Also by Jess van der Hoech

What A Muddle (2016) ISBN 978 18381987 0 1 (Co-authored with Renée Potgieter Marks)
An interactive, practical workbook designed to help children who have difficulties with emotional regulation to begin to understand what is happening in their bodies. A variety of activities throughout the book enable the child to start to explore these ideas through the story of Sam, while gently encouraging them to begin to verbalise their own experiences. Carrying out the physical exercises in the book can promote changes in emotional regulation. The text is written in a child-friendly, gender-neutral style, and is easy to understand for parents, carers and practitioners alike. For children aged 4-12.

These Three Words (2018) ISBN 978 18381987 5 6
Also available as an e-book. A unique therapeutic novel for teenagers with the aim of linking together the feelings, emotions and behaviours connected to anxiety, with some of the therapeutic tools that can be used in order to enable better self-regulation, increased confidence and different ways of thinking. The book is equally valuable to parents of teenagers with anxiety, giving them an insight and understanding into some of the issues that may be affecting their child, and potentially opening up a line of communication and a way forward between parent and teen.

These Three Words: The Journal (2019) ISBN 978 18381987 2 5
A thought-provoking and hands-on workbook, combining a series of practical exercises and tools designed to assist teenagers who are struggling with the symptoms of anxiety. Addressing the anxious responses in both brain and body, this journal provides the reader with the opportunity to discover therapeutic coping techniques and learn how to apply them to their own personal problem areas, before committing to a twenty-eight-day practice to promote good emotional regulation and reduced anxiety. The journal can be used alongside the therapeutic novel These Three Words, or as a standalone workbook, and it is suitable for use by the teenage reader on their own, with a parent, or in a group.

Beastie, Baby and the Brand-New Mummy (2022) ISBN 978 18381987 3 2 and *Beastie, Baby and the Brand-New Daddy (2022) ISBN 978 18381987 4 9*
A therapeutic story that looks at the external signs of pathological dissociation in a child. Dolly's story helps children who have experienced early trauma to begin to understand, in a very simple way, what dissociation is and why it has happened in their internal world. Tools and techniques are included within the story that parents and caregivers can use to assist the child in the first stages of their healing process. Beautiful illustrations on every page enhance the story of Dolly, and help the reader to relate to the events that happen, to notice the methods Dolly has developed to manage her feelings, and to think about what is happening in their own internal world. For children aged 4-12

Printed in Great Britain
by Amazon